Blood Fifties

Reminiscences of a itter at Laira

MIKE WOODHOUSE
Edited by Andy Griffiths

All proceeds to the Class 50 Society Preservation Fund

ISBN 0-9509354-2-5

Published by : Fearless Publications, 23 Chestnut Drive, LEIGH, Lancs. WN7 3JW

Printed by : Ryton Typing Services, Ryton Street, WORKSOP, Notts.

CONTENTS

Forward

Most of us only ever get to play with trains: Mike Woodhouse is different – it is his job to maintain and repair locomotives at a major BR depot. He is a man perfectly content with his lot, and is more than willing to share with the rest of us his enthusiasm for keeping the Class 50s running. Over the years Mike has frequently gone out of his way to help the Class 50 Society; and it is a great privilege for me to help edit his reminscences of working on these cantankerous but magnificent thoroughbreds – as seen from the perspective of one who has been involved with them throughout their entire history on the Western Region. These stories give those of us stuck on the other side of the railway fence a rare glimpse as to what goes on behind the scenes.

Mike was born in Ruislip, Middlesex, of Cornish parents in 1944. After leaving school, aged 15, he went to work for BR at Old Oak Common depot, also spending periods based at Southall and Ranelagh Bridge (Paddington) Servicing Points. In 1965 he married and two years later moved to Plymouth – not far from the foot of the infamous Hemerdon Bank – and transferred to Laira depot, where as a Train and Rolling Stock Fitter he is still employed today. During this time he has worked on most types of Western steam locos; the gas turbine prototype; the Diesel-Hydraulics from Warships to Westerns; as well as the profusion of Diesel-Electric types, inlcuding the Blue Pullman.

I for one am Brunswick-green with envy. And how many of us can say that our work is also our hobby?

Andy Griffiths
Exeter, July 1990

All photographs (unless stated) have been taken by Andy Griffiths at Laira on Tuesday 3rd July 1990.

(Front Cover) Five Class 50s line up outside Laira Depot on 24th May 1991. From left to right they are D400; 50007; 50031; 50003 and 50015. Each locomotive has a distinctive livery. *(Chris Holland)*

(Rear Cover) Mike props up 50048 'Dauntless'.

(Above) A general view of Laira from the housing estate on the hillside to the north.

(Below) The view of Laira depot from Lipson Curve.

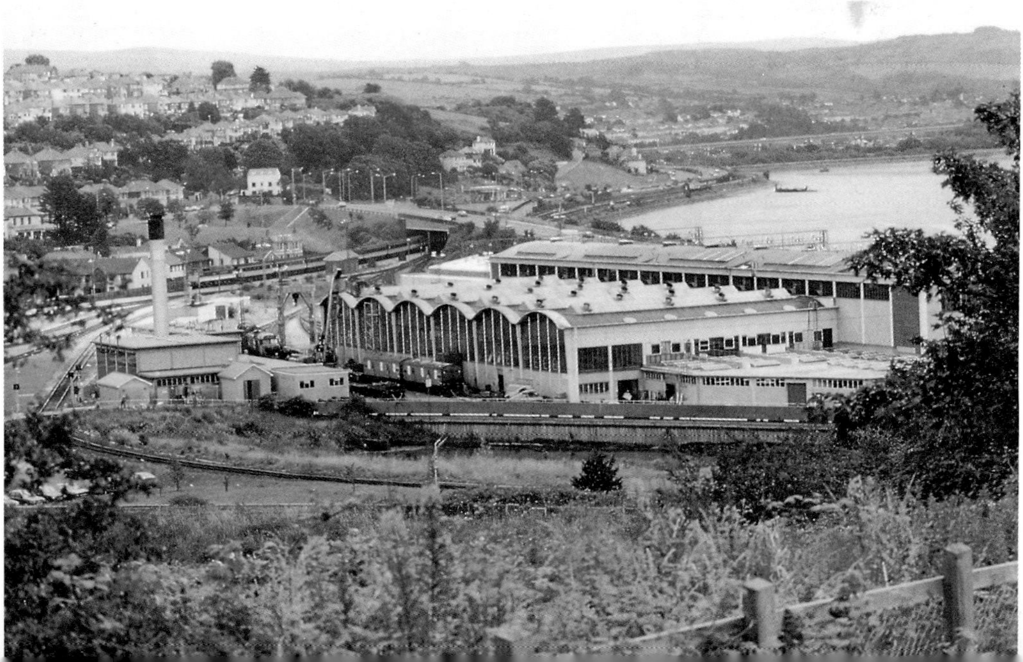

D400 comes to Plymouth

Anyone who has worked for British Rail over the last 25 years will have seen many changes in the locomotive fleet. Enginemen, engineers and management alike have had to adapt – particularly so if you were a Western Region man. This region of the BR system has always been different from the rest, not least its adoption of diesel-hydraulic traction, whereas the others went straight from steam to diesel-electric. Even today some claim the Western made the right choice.

Laira depot, at Plymouth in the heart of the Western region, has likewise seen many changes. It was one of the first diesel depots to be completed in the country, and it is also the only one to have been home to seven varieties of Type 4 locomotive, though not all at the same time. For the record these were Classes 41/42/43/46/47/50/52. The last to arrive was, of course, the Class 50.

Outside the old servicing shed (where the new HST depot has since been built) there was a short loco spur known as the sand road. It was normally used by visiting motive power or failures. A further use was to accommodate new types being used for train crew and workshop familiarisation. At this time the elimination of the hydraulics was in progress; the last 63xx out of Swindon, 6319, was already laid up.Replacement for the Type 2s, the Class 25 diesel-electric, was represented by 5179 in use for crew training purposes. 5827 soon followed, still in green with double white arrows.

It was 1973 when another stranger was due to come west, this time as a replacement for our Class 52 'Westerns'. Enter the English Electric Class 50, or D400's as they were in the original numbering. D400 first visited Laira in July 1973, on loan from Bristol Bath Road for both driver and engineer training. It reposed on the sand road and over the following months was swapped several times for 401, minus its D prefix. After one such changeover 400 returned as 50050. D402 had been visiting Old Oak Common for the same reason.

Now, it takes time to adjust to change, and when we learned that the D400s were to replace our trusty 1000s we were not happy. Officially it was put across that the new type would be trouble-free and require less maintenance. Unofficially we heard the LMR would be glad to see the back of them, and this did not help in the adjustment. Our first impressions confirmed why they were not wanted in the North: the interiors were filthy, no place for crawling around in like monkeys whilst fault finding. The inertia (non) filters were particularly bad. Another feature we did not like was that the door handles moved up to open the door, not pushed down as on other types, which is so much easier when your hands are full of tools and a hand lamp. This would not have been too bad but there were so many internal doors and the interior lighting was poor.

To the electricians they were a nightmare. Although we did have a few diesel-electrics already, the 25s and 46s, compared to a hydraulic which only had pump failure and earth faults to be dealt with, the 50s were something different. There was an electronic control system instead of the older style electro-mechanical or pneumatic, plus subsystems for slow speed control, current limiting and rheostatic braking. I remember spending a day on this braking system, the ultimate in braking, and only fitted to this diesel class. The main generators and traction motors also had to be understood. No-one at Laira had much knowledge of electronics on locos at the time, and so the CM&EE's representatives had to help out with repairs.

On the other hand, the train crews certainly liked them on first impressions. To the drivers they were fast and powerful and also rode well. Unlike the Westerns, though, which had double bulkheads between driver and engines, they were noisier and less comfortable in the cabs, and the seats were set too low.

Our first allocation of a Class 50 at Laira was 50003 at the start of April 1974. At this stage many of the depot staff shied away from working on the new locos, preferring to stick to the familiar 'Western's. It was not surprising that the feeling towards the EE Type 4's was "give us a Class 52 any day". On arrival 50003 required a 'D' exam, which is quite an in-depth maintenance programme. This would really test our knowledge of how the loco worked! 03 was berthed on No. 6 road against the stop blocks – and seemed to stay there for ages, whilst several 52s were called in for the exam and returned back to traffic. I began to wonder if Fifty would ever turn a wheel again, the old joke for locos like this being to put grass cuttings under the wheels. But to be fair, all the staff had to start from scratch in getting to grips with these maintenance schedules, finding the right location on the loco, and then working out the best way of tackling the various jobs in practice. The management were in the dark, and the stores supply was nil - parts having to be requested from Crewe, Bath Road or Old Oak.

As more of the Class came to the Western more problems came to light, the dynamic braking system becoming an especial headache. But as always the Western found its own solutions, including the refurbishment programme of the early 1980's.

And now, with the timetable changes in May 1990, Laira is home to all of the remaining Class 50s.

Westerns lose out to Hoovers

To many enthusiasts the year 1973/4 saw the beginning of the decline of the Western Region, as the withdrawal of the hugely popular Class 52 diesel-hydraulic began. Many of today's Fifty fans were weaned on bashing 'Westerns' overnight to the West Country. The days of the 50 v 52 rivalry had begun; as had the takeover by the former of the latter's work, starting with passenger turns.

In February 1975 the WR decided to abandon steam heating and thus remove loco boilers. This left the 52s with just parcels, milk, stone and general freight diagrams. 1975 was also to be the last year for Westerns on summer Saturday holiday services, with the plan being for only thirty to remain in traffic by the year end. Tandem workings of both types could be seen that summer, and two examples on Newquay holiday trains I remember were 1003 'Western Venturer' and 50043, and 50005 and 1056 'Western Sultan'.

During the early part of 1975 an industrial dispute at Bristol Bath Road over bonus payments for working on Class 50s saw many out of service. Thus although the 'Golden Hind' Plymouth to Paddington and return executives train was booked for a pair of 50s, in practice often only one was available. In consequence Class 52 substitutions could be found and on the 2nd of April 1005 'Western Venturer' worked both up and down trains. At the same time all Paddington Class 1 commuter services were in 'Western' hands, besides the clay and milk traffic.

Despite this minor revival, the overall trend was clearly in favour of the 'Hoovers'. As evidence for this, on 12th April 1975 50016 was transferred from Bath Road to Laira, causing the withdrawal of 1006 and 1050. But the 52s still had their moments. On 5th June a derailment at St. Austell blocking both lines meant that 1036, 1041 and 50028 were trapped in the far west and had to work a shuttle service to and from Penzance for a while. A more typical memory is of 1041 'Western Prince' tackling Dainton bank on one engine, but despite a gallant effort stalling and having to be rescued by 50039.

1976 saw the arrival of HSTs for the Paddington to Bristol services, releasing 'Hoovers' for the West Country traffic. By the start of February 32 'Whizzos' remained, but from then onwards BR announced there would be no diagrammed work for the class. The writing was clearly on the wall. Two weeks later 1058 'Western Nobleman' was allocated on 1A09 Penzance to Paddington, consisting of steam heating stock, but the machine was removed at Plymouth in favour of ETH-only 50047! Also about this time 50045 reached Laira from Crewe, but it lacked the ETH facility as its wiring was in such a poor condition.

There was a notable occurrence on 14th April 1976 when 1065 'Western Consort' plus 50009 worked the 1440 Plymouth to Paddington throughout. On 2nd June 50019 was derailed at Reading on the up 'Cornish Riviera Express', and the following day 1070 'Western Gauntlet' had custody of the train. The summer is now upon us, and with a continuing high level of Fifty failures, there are not infrequent Class 52 substitutions. Not that the 'Westerns' had an easy ride. On a September night 1028 'Western Hussar' was booked on the 2110 Penzance to Paddington sleeper; but at Truro it came to a complete and silent stand, and so an SOS was sent out. By chance, 50014 was stabled inside St. Blazey's little old shed and so it was duly despatched to the rescue. On nearing the stranded train the 50 was switched wrong-line in order to buffer up, but as it was dark and the sleeper had stopped on a severe curve, 50014 smacked into 1028. The rusting nose of 'Western Hussar' caved in, and the loco was withdrawn as the result, but 50014 was only superficially damaged.

superficially damaged.

At the start of 1976 eight Class 50s were still based on their native LMR, by the mid summer all had migrated to the Western Region. There was now nothing much for the 52s to do. Six remained by the end of 1976, and the final day came on 26th February 1977, leaving the field clear for the Fifties to establish themselves and develop a following.

Headcode Matter

During the dieselisation of the late 1950s British Railways Board ordered many types of locomotives from a variety of manufacturers; but they all had to be fitted with disc-type train indicators. These were white metal discs attached to each cab end and illuminated at night, in an arrangement of three across the top and one centrally below. They were hinged in the middle and so could be opened and closed, the resulting pattern identifying the type of train. This idea had been used by the SR and LMSR for many years.

However, soon after the pilot diesel locos entered service the BRB ruled in favour of a system that could identify train type, destination and number. This was the four character headcode, featuring a panel built into the cab front, or, in the case of the Fifties, at roof level above the cab windows. The first character was a number showing the class of traffic, the second letter for the destination, and the third and fourth numbers for the train number.

This system lasted some sixteen years, but was dropped on 1st January 1976, mainly due to the introduction of the TOPS computer control, but also because of the disappearance of signal boxes and passing loops making identification en route unnecessary. Depots throughout the BR system were told to fix the headcode panel to read 0000. However, on the Western the loco number was allowed to be shown in the panel instead. At Laira the Class 52s were all so treated, the only exception being 1023 'Western Fusilier'. On 18th November 1976 it was being made ready for a special from Kings Cross to York two days later, the 'Western Talisman' tour. The indicator blind was torn and so I obtained permission to fit the G39 'eyes' plastic strip with two white circles to permit backlighting. Later this was fitted as standard to all locos.

Many Fifties also carried their number, minus one zero, especially the ones allocated to Bath Road and Old Oak; but usually only for a short period before the G39 modification was carried out during the exam programme. 50030 was the last of the class to retain a working headcode panel. As an experiment the headcode boxes on 50003 and 50035 were panelled over, with lamps mounted in the plating, So too was 50007, but at the end only, repair being needed due to accident damage.

During heavy repair (generally refurbishment) at Doncaster Works all headcode boxes were covered over, as many were leaking water through onto the driver's desk.Despite the fitting of the high-intensity headlight the two backlit 'eyes' were and still are retained.

Nameplates Ahoy!

During the summer of 1977 the Western region management made the decision to name all of the Class 50 fleet. In keeping with the tradition of naming locos with naval connections, the 50s were to be called 'Warships', as had the earlier diesel-hydraulic Classes 41/42/43. Many of the names had previously been carried by LMS steam 'Jubilees'. Although the appellation 'Warships' did not stick, the names themselves have helped greatly to boost the popularity of the Fifties.

Any enthusiast visiting Laira loco stores at Christmas 1977 would have had a treat indeed, in the form of seeing one hundred gleaming red-and-silver cast nameplates, fresh from the presses at Swindon. At the time the names had not been assigned to individual locos, and it was my job to label each plate when the decision was made. We had the task of fitting plates not just to our own allocation, but also to the six based at Bristol Bath Road. A few naming ceremonies were planned, but in most cases the plates were fixed without fuss at the depot.

First to escape from anonymity was 50035. An invitation had been sent to the Navy for the naming of '35 as 'Ark Royal', since it was anticipated that the famous aircraft carrier (based at Plymouth Devonport) would shortly be sailing on her last commission. The previous railbound owner of the name had been D601 – also based at Laira, and also one of the depot's favourites. During early January 1978 50035 came onto the depot for a complete external repaint, cabs included, plus the requisite 'C' exam. I was involved with all this, and with the management we tried to work out the measurements for fitting the plates from the drawings that Swindon had sent us.

January 16th was the day that the first nameplate was actually attached. It was no easy task. The main problem was how to trace up the height and centre of the body. We measured other 50s but they were all slightly different. Eventually a template was made up square to the engine room roof bodyline. With a plate on each side any fitting that was not straight or square would be noticed at a glance. A further difficulty was the variation in plate length, from 'Indominatable' (50026) to 'Lion' (50027). In the end a centre tap hole was drilled, adjustments being made with the one bolt before final fixing. A final touch was to remove the oval 'English Electric Leasing Company' plates, if the loco still carried them.

I must admit that seeing 50035 'Ark Royal' for the first time created a new impression on me: from now on it would have a character of its own. A further distinction was the fitting of white headcode panel lamps. The naming ceremony was then performed the next day by Captain Anson of HMS 'Ark Royal' at Plymouth North Road station. I believe that today's 'Ark' carries in its messroom a nameplate from D601 and a crest from 50035.

From then on I was involved with the naming of all but the last two of the class to be treated – but more about these later. In the meantime the other 98 plates lay gathering dust in a corner of the stores, as two full months elapsed before the next namings took place. This came about due to a request from RPPR Railtours for two 'namers' for their 'Derby Double' tour on 18th March. At the same time HMS 'Dauntless', the shore establishment near Reading, expressed an interest in a naming ceremony. This tied in well, since 50048, the loco booked for the name 'Dauntless', was due for an 'E' exam and full repaint. 50010 was also on the maintenance exam programme so this too would receive its name, 'Monarch'.

The pair duly emerged from Laira in the early hours of the 16th resplendent with their new names. Both headed east light engines to Old Oak, '48 later going to Reading for its naming ceremony. 50035 plus 50048 were booked for the doubleheader from Paddington to Derby, with 50010 as standby; but in the event 'Ark Royal' refused to operate in multiple with 'Dauntless' and so '48 and '10 worked the train.

From this date onwards I would take a note of each Class 50 coming on for repair at Laira and then go and ask the Chief Mechanical Engineer if he would agree to the nameplates being fitted. Of course, some locos were in Doncaster Works at this period, and the Bristol six (50039–044) were hard to remove from traffic. Sometimes it would only be one, sometimes two, but on 6th April no less than three 'Warships' were named: 50018 as 'Resolution', 50034 'Furious', and 50007 'Hercules' – a loco later to be surrounded by controversy over its name.

As it turned out, April 1978 saw the naming on no less than sixteen of the class: from then on it became a steady flow. Only after twenty had been done did we get our hands on the first of the Bath Road allocation, when on April 26th 50044 became 'Exeter'. May was also a busy month, the namings tally moving on to 33, the last being 50014 'Warspite' on the 30th. This name had last been carried by 'Jubilee' Class 4–6–0 number 45724.

By mid summer only a few were left unnamed. On August 4th the ex D400, 50050, became 'Fearless'; but at the last moment the Navy decided to have a naming ceremony, and so the plates were removed on the 7th and put back in the stores. Finally a suitable date for the ceremony was arranged, and on the afternoon of the 23rd 50050 was officially twinned with its naval namesake, the formalities taking place at the depot itself.

From then on the flow of namings became a trickle. No more were done in August, but on 1st September my own 50008 acquired the name 'Thunderer'. Six were left without names; of these, two were away at Doncaster Works, and two were Bath Road based. These two were caught first; 50040 arriving for tyre turning on September 15th and becoming 'Leviathan', and 50042 receiving its 'Triumph' plates some three weeks later.

My final loco was 50029, which on 14th November emerged as 'Renown'. The other two were still on 'The Plant' at Doncaster, 50006 as the prototype for refurbishment, and 50011 undergoing classified repair. '11 was outshopped in April 1979 with a new power unit, but without any treatment to the bodyside, which was very rough. It ran around in service until being made 'Centurion' on 20th August 1979. Meanwhile, the 'Neptune' plates for '06 had transferred north to Donny on 20th June, but the exact date of fitting is not certain. Whenever, it was the only Fifty to be named on the Eastern Region, finally entering traffic as 'Neptune' on 15th December 1979 – 49th to be named, but 50th and last to run in service (and also the only unrefurbished class member not to receive a name). Ironically these two locos were last to be named but first to be withdrawn.

Hercules III

This story concerns the third locomotive of the British Railways fleet to carry the name 'Hercules'. The first was the 4–6–0 steam loco 45703 of the London Midland Region; the second D822, a Western Region hydraulic built at Swindon in 1960.Just seven years later the frames were laid at Newton-le-Willows in Lancashire for the third 'Hercules'. D407 emerged anonymous, just another 100 mph D400 Class for use between Crewe and Scotland; but today the loco has become the flagship of the Western fleet. To paraphrase a well-known saying: 'they seek him here, they seek him there, they seek 'Sir Edward Elgar' everywhere!'

D407 was allocated from its native LMR to the WR at Laira in April 1974, one of the first to be transferred. Soon afterwards it was renumbered 50007. In 1974 it suffered serious damage to the cab at No. 1 end whilst shunting at Bristol: I can remember the managers talking to the welders and sheet metalworkers to see if Laira could undertake the repair. In the event two of my workmates proved that it could, '07 being berthed on No. 5 road stop blocks and the cab stripped out. Gradually the nose was brought back into shape. One of our welders had worked in the RN dockyard at Devonport, and for him the work was easy when compared to patching up a ship.

At last the work was done, this being the biggest job ever achieved on Laira depot. Even today the scars of the job can still be seen, notably on the buffer beam: but '07 still lives.

The name 'Hercules' was applied on 6th April 1978, the eleventh of the class to be named. Nearly five years later the loco emerged from the refurbishment programme in the new large-logo livery, 35th to be treated, but still just one of the crowd.

1984 changed all that. Early in the year it was announced that 50007 was to be renamed 'Sir Edward Elgar' and repainted in GWR brunswick green, in connection with the 50th anniversary of the composer's death, and as a prelude to the Great Western 150th anniversary celebrations. Much controversy surrounded the move: some enthusiasts were outraged, and the affair even reached the local newspapers. Whatever the rights and wrongs (for example the appropriateness of having 49 naval 50s and one musician), the decision stood.

The conversion process was swift, as the official naming ceremony was to take place at Paddington on 25th February. At 1600 hours on Wednesday 8th '07 lost its 'Hercules' nameplates, to be sold at Collector's Corner in Euston. By Saturday the loco had been given a suitable undercoat for its pre-war green livery, the top coat being applied the following day, the Sunday. On Monday the roof was painted black, as were the bogies on Tuesday, and the buffer beam in red on Wednesday. The lining out was completed on Thursday 16th, with the next three days being occupied by bogie repairs and painting the inside of the cabs. The brass GWR-style numberplates were attached on the Friday and the nameplates on the following Monday. After inspection the new-look '07 left Laira for Old Oak at 0005 hours on Tuesday 21st.

Simon Rattle of the Birmingham Symphony Orchestra unveiled the 'Sir Edward Elgar' plaques on the appointed day, which was marred only by persistent traction motor problems. Since then '07 has become very well known, travelling the BR system to attend numerous Open Days. In 1985/6, for example, it visited Birkenhead, Canon Street, Carlisle, Coalville and Landore – to name but a few.

In March 1987 an 'F' exam was carried out on 'Sir Edward', but the loco was not repainted. Two years later sectorisation meant that 50007 had to join the NSSA fleet in the Network SouthEast stable, which meant that a repaint into the standard livery was required. However, a decision came down from on high that a dispensation would be granted for '07 to retain its brunswick green livery, as a special 'thank you' from Network SouthEast to the Laira staff for keeping the Fifties running.So it was that a full repaint was undertaken in time for the 21st anniversary of the BR Staff Association club at Laira. '07 was presented back to the NSE fleet, with all staff – past and present – attending the ceremony. All the Depot Engineers from the 1960s to the 1990s helped to plant a tree of dedication.

50007 was well and truly Laira's flagship. As a footnote, the present fleet manager is an ex-Eastern Region man, and so '07 carries the embellishment 'Laira' on its buffer beams – after the Kings Cross 'top shed' tradition.

50040's Double Life

The first part of this tale dates back to 1981. After return to the WR following refurbishment at Doncaster Works each Fifty would be inspected on an audit, to see if the allocated repairs had been carried out to the satisfaction of the Region's CM&EE department. Usually there was no problem, but when 50040 'Leviathan' returned home shiny in its new large-logo livery in July 1981 the technical staff at Laira concluded that BREL's costings were not justified. The 'phone lines between Laira, Paddington (the WR headquarters) and Doncaster were red hot, until at last the Works accepted '40 for rectificatiron.

Coincidently, F&W Railtours were about to run their 'Doncaster Dart' tour from Plymouth to Doncaster Works, and it was partly at my suggestion that it would be a good idea to take '40 back to Donny via this train. Arrangements were made and accepted. Thus it was the gricers (AG among them) that were privileged to have superpower in the form of 50025 plus 50040 for the northwards leg of the tour, on 26th July. The 5,400 h.p. duo put in a splendid performance, appreciated by all. '40 was back on the WR within a fortnight, this time behaving satisfactorily. Sadly, both locos have now been withdrawn.

The second part takes place eight years on, in the twilight of 50040's life. In 1987 '40 was rechristened 'Centurion', because 50011, which had carried the plates, had been taken out of service for use as a power unit test bed at Crewe Works. This was an embarrassment to BR since a twinning ceremony with HMS 'Centurion' had taken place not long beforehand; and so the plates were transferred to 50040, the 'Levithan' name no longer having a current naval association.

Anyway, on this particular day, 31st July 1989, I was out evaluating Eastfield-based 37188, on test following its 'G' overhaul at Laira. We ran light engine to Par in Cornwall, where on arrival our driver was asked by the signalman if we would go to Burngullow clay sidings. We all agreed and so he dropped the arm of the Par station starter and we powered away. At Burngullow the shunter said there were some clay slurry tankers to manoeuvre, and some defective ones to take back to St. Blazey depot.

This we duly did. It has always amazed me that whatever the time of day and wherever you are there is always a rail enthusiast hanging around with a camera. Today was no exception, and as we approached Par once more I glimpsed a cameraman dashing from one side of the road overbridge to the other as we crawled up to the signal. From his figure I seemed to recognise him: truly, it was an old mate of mine from Lancashire. We exchanged tal by shouting in between shunting movements. 37188 was uncoupled and ran round the tanks before proceeding up the Newquay branch to back into the St. Blazey Carriage and Wagon Yard.

On being released we ran back light to Par, where DCWA (Departmental sector) 50040 had just arrived on the Mondays-only 6M22 train, the 1305 Truro to Ince & Elton fertiliser working.Was this the last stand in Cornwall for '40? Both locos stood side by side: the Class 37 spotless, the Class 50 looking very rough, its engine emitting blue smoke – a sure sign of heavy engine wear. I was about to suggest that we went on front to assist, but the lower quadrant starter dropped to give '40 the road. The 50 coughed out of Par with 6M22, leaving the station blanketed in smoke. I commented to the driver that we might have to give rear-end assistance to the train up Largin Bank; but when we were finally given the road there was no delay, and we passed '40 waiting in the through road at Plymouth station.

This was indeed the last stand for 50040 in Cornwall. Within three weeks the loco was taken out of service and never ran again. At the time of writing it lies cannibalised at Laira with sister 50010, waiting to be cut up.

Dawn of a new image

It is the 4th September 1980, and I'm on the early morning duty. The sun peeked over the roof line: a fine summer's day lay ahead. In the foreman's office the buzz was that 50023 'Howe' had been delivered back from Doncaster after refurbishment – but sporting a bold new livery (unlike the first six to be treated). After receiving the day's work load most of us gathered outside on the oil road. A gleaming 'Howe' stood before us, resplendent in the 'new image' of wrap-round yellow cabs, grey roof, and large logo and number. Most pleasing to the eye; especially after the many years of the drab all-over blue livery (carried by all the 50s since new).

During the day most of the Laira staff, from CME to office workers, came out to admire the novel paint scheme. As the sun rose further in the sky the loco shone, and many photographs were taken. Of course, many Eastern Region railfans had already seen the new-look '23 on its test runs and on 1V93, the 0905 Edinburgh to Plymouth, booked for a Deltic to York where the Fifty would take over in order to return home to the WR and Laira. This duty was often used as a means of getting freshly-outshopped 50s back to their own territory.

For a while 50023 became Laira's flagship, just as D1023 'Western Fusilier' had been half a decade earlier. The Fifty celebrated its unique status by working the return leg of the RPPR 'Mayflower' railtour from Plymouth to Paddington later in the month.

Within four years '23 was once more standard in appearance as all the Class had been repainted in the large logo livery. But, in 1986, 'Howe' again led the way when it was joint first to sport the Network South East colours.
(although it will probably return to Laira in the May 1990 timetable change), and carries the revised, darker blue NSE livery. Any further livery change is most unlikely; and so the only question that remains is will it, like its numbersake D1023, be the last in traffic and end up being preserved? We shall have to wait and see.

50016 'Barham' Destined to be withdrawn two weeks later.

Why 50149?

1986 witnessed the rise of Network South East and its distinctive red-white-and-blue livery. Most of the 50s were destined to end up in this garb, but some of the other newly-formed sectors were also responsible for a share of the work performed by the Class. With effect from the New Year of 1987 "it was rumoured" Railfreight would take over responsibility for ten locos. They were to form a sub-class, 50/1, and be numbered 50101 to 50110. Arrangements were put in hand for the modification work to be done at BREL Doncaster Works. In the meantime no maintenance to the electric train heating equipment on the selected locos was to be allowed, and all operating expenses were to be charged to Railfreight.

The locomotives chosen were 50001/003/005/010/012/015/022/024/050, with the tenth still to be decided. However, it quickly became apparent that the gang of nine were not dedicated to freight work, but used just the same as the rest of the Class.

In April 1987 Railfreight sector confirmed it would put up the money to modify the first unit. The selected loco would be one from the 'F' overhaul programme then underway at Laira, and all the work would be undertaken by the depot itself. In terms of modifications required, the 50/1 was to have regeared Class 37 wheelsets and traction motors, a derating adjustment to the power unit, and disconnection of the ETH apparatus.

So, which 50 would it be? 50050/028/044/049/043/005 was the provisional running order for the summer overhaul programme. As with all heavy maintenance to the 'Hoovers' I was actively involved, and played a part in each of the 23 'F' exams that Laira did. It was not until July that the regeared bogies were delivered, and what with staff shortages plus 50050 (just starting its exam) requiring new bogies, it seemed that 'Fearless' would become 50101 – or would it be 50150?

However, it was not to be. After some delay '50 was given ordinary bogies and entered the Network SouthEast fleet; and so the honour fell to the next in line, which happened to be 50049 'Defiance'. Railfreight and the engineers from the Derby research HQ were pushing for a September release to traffic for trials, and so work began in earnest. '49 was birthed on No. 6 road stop blocks, and as well as the internal changes it was also to have the new Railfreight livery: Laira staff were to witness yet another new image. If the experiment was a success then this might be a lifeline for some classmembers not down on the 'F' programme and thus facing early retirement.

In early September 50049 finally gave way to 50149, repainted in three-tone grey with the distinctive red-and-yellow chequer of the Railfreight General sub-sector. A first for Laira was having its own depot badge cast – of a ship, what else! By the required date of 20th September all the finishing touches were complete and '149 was handed over to the Derby engineers. The Class 50/1 made its first trial run light engine to Totnes and back in the early afternoon of the 22nd.

Its first real test came the next day on the afternoon shift. 47019, in charge of 6B43, the 1425 St. Blazey to Severn Tunnel Junction Speedlink freight, came light from Tavistock Junction Yard in order to collect 'Defiance' for testing. In the meantime the payload of the train had been made up to 960 tonnes. This proved almost too much for '149 and its derated 2,400 h.p. power unit on the 1 in 42 of Hemerdon bank, as it very nearly stalled; but worse was to come.

I was working on the next 'F' exam loco, 50043, when the call came through that '149 was off the road at Exeter. On being informed of the news I just could not believe it, but the foreman then came and told me and the rest of the breakdown gang to clear up what we were doing and make our way to the breakdown train. Our information was that 50149, 47019 and the leading wagon of the train had been derailed in Riverside Yard: a long shift was ahead.

50029 'Renown' was provided to power the breakdown train, and good progress was made to Exeter.We pulled up alongside the derailment and got out to examine the damage. The two locos were going to be an easy lift as one bogie of each had just dropped off the road in a straight line. 'Defiance' was the first to be rerailed, and once this was achieved I climbed aboard to restart the engine. As we waited for the air brake pressure to build the bogie was examined and the decision taken to bring '149 home with us. '29 ran round and jumpered up to the 50/1, and then recoupled the breakdown unit.

Next came 47019, and as it was being rerailed the rest of 6B43 was shunted into an adjacent siding. By the time the loaded 75-tonne 'Tiger' clay wagon was back on the rails and our job complete it was the early hours of the next morning; at last we and the 50s could return to Laira.

The official Railfreight launch was not until 15th October, with adhesion trials planned the following weekend between Westbury and Warminster. Alas, disaster struck on the 8th, when '149 suffered a major engine failure at Yatton. 50014, working the Waterloo to Exeter route that day, was taken out of traffic to supply a replacement power unit (This being the last Fifty left with untreated mainframe fractures, 50006/011 already been withdrawn). 'Warspite' was later scrapped as a result. By working round the clock '149 was restored to health in time, but the trials were not a great success. No more 50/1s were authorised, and after eighteen months 'Defiance' was converted back to standard 50049 and returned to passenger work.

A winter's tale.

In the winter of 1981/82 many parts of Britain suffered blizzard conditions, from the north of Scotland right down to Cornwall. Heavy snow and ice everywhere caused British Rail services to be in chaos, but running wherever possible. The West Country was no exception. Laira was virtually besieged by all types of motive power and coaching stock suffering from a variety of freeze-up troubles. This story starts, however, further north and features 50030 'Repulse', still unrefurbished and in Rail Blue livery.

Whilst working a Paddington to Worcester service in whiteout conditions 50030 became a casualty with power earth faults due to snowy and generally damp conditions. Eventually it became stuck, and with a storm raging an SOS was sent for assistance. At the time '30 was only one of many locos similarly affected, from class 31s to HST power cars. After quite a while the train was rescued, but for poor old 'Repulse' it was only a beginning. Because of general chaos the loco was dumped in the open at Worcester and left to shiver over the weekend in sub-zero conditions.

It was decided to tow the stricken Fifty to Gloucester, but on arrival there neither they or Bath Road could provide attention as both had more than enough similar work to cope with already. So together with two Class 47s, two Class 37s and a Class 31 it was despatched home to Laira. On arrival '30 was berthed in No. 5 road to thaw out and have its faults diagnosed. It took two days before work could be started, so bad was the freezing-up.

The first check was on the cooler group. This showed all four radiator banks plus header tank needing to be replaced. After completing this work attention turned to the power unit, and here the diagnosis was failure of three turbochargers, two intercoolers, the water pump, many cylinder heads and all the water hoses and flexible couplings. Three weeks and many man-hours later the weather was back to normal, but not so 50030; the work seemed to be endless!

A final attempt was made to make the engine watertight. The engine and radiator were refilled and I turned the key to restart '30's power unit for the first time in a month: after all this time it was good to see light at the end of the tunnel. The engine was left to idle and became nicely warmed up, only for it to shut down without warning. A check on the radiator gauge showed it to be empty. A steady top up was made and the engine restarted; this time an inch by inch survey of the engine block revealed a hairline fracture. After all that effort this was to be the end: nothing further could be done (this being in the days before Laira had the facilities to exchange power units), and so the loco was shipped off to Works for repair. Curiously, although the refurbishment programme was well over half way complete, 50030 was not included at this juncture.

Mike poses with his favourite Fifty, 50008 'Thunderer'

Hard day's night.

It is Friday the 31st of August 1984; the time is 10.30 pm. For most people it is the end of the working week and the end of the day, but for those of us on the night shift at Laira the hard graft is just about to start. It is clear but mild summer's night, still with a lingering reminder of the heat of the day. I book on for duty, and after changing into overalls I'm ready for work.

The Servicing Shed Foreman informs me that tonight I will be working mainly on Class 50s: seven are awaiting attention, together with one Class 45 and one Class 47. It should be borne in mind that there are two departments concerned with keeping locos running at a depot such as Laira, namely Traffic and Movements plus the CMEE (Chief Mechanical and Electrical Engineer – in other words, repair and maintenance). Both must work hand in hand to achieve optimum results.

After collecting my tools and lamps I make my way to No. 4 road in the main shed. The work will be carried out by a gang of two fitters, one electrician and a mate. 47053 is on the fuelling point topping up with only 26 gallons of fuel; while this is in progress I make a quick detour to survey the scene in the rest of the shed. There are seven Fifties out of service, these being:-

No. 1 road : 50032 (OC), on jacks for a double bogie change;
No. 4 road : 50021 (OC), flashover repair to main generator;
No. 5 road : 50014 (LA), 'B' exams;
No. 6 road : 50012 (LA), 'B' exam;
: 50017 (LA), repair to ETH generator;
Outside : 50015 (LA), await transfer to Doncaster Works;
Cleaning shed : 50044 (LA), 'B' exam.

Now it's back to my night's work, which will consist mainly of footplate checks and the basic 'A' exam to seven Fifties, most of which are already allocated to work trains the next morning. These are:-

50048 (LA), 'A' exam, booked on Turn 213b:
0538 Plymouth to Penzance (2357 ex-Paddington),
1105 Penzance to Paddington, etc.
50046 (LA), 'A' exam, booked on Turn 211c:
0707 Plymouth to Paignton empty stock,
0945 Paignton to Paddington, etc.
50019 (LA), FP exam, booked on Turn 220b:
0405 Laira to Exeter empty stock,
0548 Exeter to Waterloo, etc.
50016 (LA), FP exam, booked on Turn 221b:
0540 Laira to Newton Abbot staff train and local to Exeter,
0813 Exeter to Waterloo, etc.
50025 (OC), FP exam, booked on Turn 205d:
0608 Laira to Paignton empty stock,
0855 Paignton to Paddington, etc.
50045 (LA), FP exam, spare: confied to local duties,
awaiting transfer to Doncaster Workes for classified repair.
50010 (LA), due to arrive with loss of coolant problems.

These locos would clock up over a thousand miles between them whilst hauling the Summer Saturday holiday traffic, and it is our responsibility to see that they perform it without any mishap. It will be a busy night.

47053 has now come on to the pit for its inspection. 50048 draws up to take fuel, and as it has been out on the road for some time it takes on 745 gallons. The whole area is lit up by tower arc lamps making it just like daylight. 50046/016/010 have already arrived, and, engines running, are waiting for their turn at the fuelling point. My mate and I start on 50048's 'A' exam, and though not long back in service it looks a little grubby. I do the bogie examination first and note that all the brakes need adjustment. I then join my mate in the cab for a full brake test and engine run-up. Meanwhile 50046 has drawn up and proceeds to fill up with 270 gallons of diesel. I give the movements men the all-clear for 47053 and 50048, and as it is now midnight we have a drink of tea while the two locos are moved out and replaced by '46.

On our return nothing has happened, the locos are in the same place as before. The reason is that the shunt crew on 08895 are busy drawing the chained-together old bogies out from under 50032 and depositing them in the next road, followed by collecting the replacements and reversing the procedure so that the loco can be reassembled. Outside 45012 is ready for the Plymouth to Penzance parcels, and a buffet car required at Penzance is being attached. By now 'Ajax' is in place over the pit and we begin its 'A' exam. Again the brakes need adjustment and the windscreen wiper on the secondman's side is found to be broken and in need of replacement.

We are working against time, and to add to the difficulty there appears to be confusion concerning 50010, which has drawn up to take fuel: obviously the Movements side are not aware of its loss of coolant problem. In any event, 50021 is already berthed in No. 4 road, and has been there for a week with its flashover damage, meaning that space is at a premium. Therefore it is decided to concentrate on locos with booked workings later on in the day.

50025 manoeuvres up to the fuelling point, and we examine the brakes while they are on: once more adjustment is needed. In the interim 'Invincible' has taken on 260 gallons of fuel. There is still no sign of 50019 arriving back at Laira after its day's labour, yet according to the plan it should be the first to be booked off again in the morning. As we complete the checks on '25 I notice that '32 is being lowered onto its new bogies and across the other side of the shed the overhead crane is lifting the replacement ETH generator into '17.

It is now 2.30 am and we take our meal break. 50016/019/045 remain to be serviced, along with 50010 if we can find time. During our absence '25 plus '46 are shunted out and '16 plus '45 shunted in.

'Barham' takes 577 gallons of fuel and 'Achilles' 299 gallons. Looking over the former it is found that very little attention is needed, whereas the latter needs its brakes adjusting. This done I tell my mate that I will go and have a look at '10 whilst the next shunt is completed. It had arrived after piloting 50035 on the up sleeper (2135 Penzance to Paddington). I check the coolant level first and find this to be satisfactory, and so check the radiator and engine for leaks; again nothing amiss. Next I examine the radiator fan speed, as perhaps the coolant had boiled away. Once more this was not the problem, and so I return to No. 4 road where 50019 is just arriving.

As stated earlier, 'Ramillies' is booked off at 0405, but, surprise surprise, the brakes need adjusting. I decide I had better report to the foreman about both '10 and '19, as it might well prove preferable for the latter to swap duties with another 50 already available. Unfortunately this will not be possible as Movements have committed 50019 to train 5002, the e.c.s. for the first up Waterloo service. Time is not on our side and the eyes are getting a little heavy. The engine needs 25 gallons of oil, and by now the Exeter crew are standing by and have to wait for us to finish the exam.

Our foreman returns to tell us that 50010 will come in on No. 4 pit behind 50021; we will have a second look for coolant leaks. The final shunt is made and '19 leaves the shed trailing smoke, clouding the light of the shed lamps. 'Monarch' arrives, and a glance at the bogies reveals the need for a complete reblock. Again this is relayed to the foreman, who says that '10 will be stopped for further investigation.

It is now the time to write up the logs and worksheets. The TOPS computer shows that Laira's 50027 is stopped at Tyseley for derailment damage, whilst 50029 – also one of ours – is on Old Oak Common for a main generator change. It is now 5.00 am and time for a wash before booking off and going home to bed. 'Good morning, Fifty followers, I hope you all enjoy your summer Saturday travels.' Perhaps next time you will spare a thought for those nightshift men who prepared your locos for traffic.

By way of a postscript, I was picking blackberries with my family at Totnes that afternoon when the unprecedented sight of 58002 hauling a failed HST on the 12.10 Liverpool to Penzance rattled past on the nearby line. I immediately hurried back to Laira ...

Men of the Greyhounds

This is a tale of the 'Green Badge' men.

Many of our older Class 50 drivers are proud of their 'roots' on either the Western or Southern Regions. With the rise of the Sectors the old Regions have taken a back seat, but on the ground the old rivalries still exist. Both Exeter and Plymouth had SR and WR depots, deriving of course from the Great Western and London & South Western Railways. In both cases it is the WR bases that have survived, men from Exmouth Junction now working at Exeter St. Davids, and Plymouth Friary men now at Plymouth Laira. This does not deter the SR crews from flaunting their heritage as successors to the 'Green Badge' elite, who drove Bullied 'Merchant Navy' and 'West Country' Classes on the 'Atlantic Coast Express'; and, in earlier days, the Drummond 'Greyhounds'. Today the SR men have a reputation for driving rather differently from their WR colleagues: on the Waterloo route this is termed 'hard and fast'.

One Sunday morning in the summer of 1988 I had a cab ride on the 0940 Exeter to Waterloo, care of a 'Green Badge' driver and 50021 'Rodney' (based at Old Oak at the time). Our train gets the right of way and with a blast on the horn we accelerate out of St. Davids and up the steep 1 in 37 bank to Exeter Central (the erstwhile Queen Street, the SR station). The driver pushes '21 very hard, roaring off between the thirteen station stops en route. At Salisbury there used to be a crew change, but now Exeter men go through to Waterloo and back. From here the road is fast and straight, and 'Rodney' is clearly working well with the load of eight Mark 2s.

As we meet the line from Bournemouth at Worting Junction, on the edge of Basingstoke, we find we are running alongside one of the modern generation Class 442 'Wessex Electrics'. This is the first time I had seen one of these sleek new EMUs. The driver comments that we will give the unit a run for its money into Waterloo.

Honours are even under yellow signals into Basingstoke station, but we are first away from the stop. '21 is given full power to lift its train towards the 100 mph line speed limit, as the road ahead is green. I slide the co-drivers window down to have a look back, and see that the 442 is gaining on us. Despite its quicker acceleration we have the measure of it, sprinting like a Greyhound towards Woking, the final stop before the stop-go crawl into Waterloo. Even so, the EMU just manages to draw ahead, the drivers acknowledging each other.

After Woking both trains are running between sections as the track gangs were busy tidying the permanent way in preparation for the heavy Monday morning traffic. It seemed like we had lost the race, but then at Vauxhall the EMU was passed at a stand, waiting for access to its platform at the terminus. We pull up to the buffers on time.

A well earned tea break meant that our crew were refreshed to return on the 1410 down service, with Old Oak's 50036 'Victorious'. Whilst preparing for the homeward journey it was found that the loco needed coolant, and '36 had to be topped up again at Salisbury and back on St. Davids stabling point. But the 50 had accomplished its task on time, a tribute to the doughty 'Green Badge' men and their 1980's Greyhounds.

Waterloo sunset

As it is now certain that the Exeter to Waterloo line will be the last bastion of Class 50 activity, let's focus now on the route and changes of diesel motive power.

It is interesting to note that the first diesels to take the LSWR way to the South West were, like the 50s, the products of English Electric. Built in between 1950 and 1954 for the Southern Region, 10201, 10202 and 10203 pounded the rails out of Waterloo for a while, but when full dieselisation came in the 1960s it was the Maybach-engined Class 42 diesel-hydraulics that were given control of the SR services to Exeter and beyond. These Warships, some in maroon livery, some in green, and by bearing names today held by the 50s, would haul mostly Bulleid and Maunsell green-liveried stock, steam heated and vacuum braked. Newton Abbot shed (code 83A) was the base for much of this operation.

The most famous train on the route, 'The Atlantic Coast Express', last ran one September Saturday in 1964. This year also marked the downgrading of the line, surely a mistake, with stations closed and sections of line singled. In the early 1970s Newton Abbot shed closed, the work being transferred to Laira (84A, as was), and the Class 42s were phased out.

In their place came SR Class 33s, based at Stewarts Lane, Hither Green and Eastleigh. The coaching stock also changed, dual braked and dual heated Mark 2s in blue-and-grey livery. This was definitely an improvement for the traveller, but the Waterloo to Exeter line remained a secondary route.

A revival of fortunes has taken place in the 1980s, starting with the introduction of Fifty-power, reducing the schedules to the fastest since the days of the limited-stop 'ACE'. Crew training with the 50s began in 1979, involving men from Exeter, Salisbury and Eastleigh. Old Oak loaned a loco to Stewarts Lane for familiarisation at that end of the line, 50004 being the first to venture south of the Thames. Many drivers did not get on well with the Class at first, sending the locos back to the WR for attention to even the slightest defect – much to the consternation of the operating authorities.

Now the 50s have held away for a decade, showing themselves to be master of this demanding route. With them have come other improvements, such as the reopening of stations (e.g. Pinhoe and Templecombe) and the reinstatement of passing loops (e.g. Tisbury). Affairs must have been improving as one day in April 1981 50014 worked the 0910 Waterloo to Exeter service complete with an 'ACE' headboard. But it was 1986 and the arrival of Network SouthEast that has had the biggest impact – and not just in terms of being a lifeline for the Fifties. Today the route in the most prosperous it has been for many years, and with the Channel Tunnel traffic is expected to rise dramatically.

A £55 million upgrading has just been sanctioned, and so from 1992 a new form of motive power and coaching stock will be needed. 'Fearless', 'Dreadnought' and the rest have done their job well, but time is now running out for them; their Waterloo sunset is at hand.

The shells of 50040, 50020 and 50010 await the cutters torch.

Ups and Downs, Western Style

It was the October school half term in the West Country, and as as usual it was raining. On a Wednesday just before I had some leave due I was instructed to ride 50002 'Superb' to Paignton, to check on its persistent low coolant problems. Having booked on and assembled tools and snack I made my way to outside on No. 1 road at Laira. There was '02, sheltering under the bogie hoist, and in the company of 45144, 47151 and 50016.Our train was 5A48, 0810 off shed, 0840 off Laira Carriage Sidings empty stock to Paignton, to form 1A48 – the 1105 Paignton to Paddington 'Torbay Express'.

After checking the coolant level I started up 02's engine, and then had a look at the CU4 unit to make sure the radiator fan speed and radiator shutters were all functioning properly. The driver arrives, this being a single-manned turn, and after he has performed his checks we set off for the carriage sidings, the windscreen wipers flicking to and fro.

At the dummy signal 45144 is waiting to enter No. 1 sidings we also wait and then enter No. 4 road. Our train comprises eight assorted Mark 2s. Whilst we couple on and perform the brake test the Class 45 does the same over on its air conditioned stock, which will form the 1105 Plymouth to Newcastle. The ETH button is depressed to warm the train en route, and then revs up 'Superb's engine before applying power and threading out of the sidings.

Using 1,000 amps we cross the down main line, and on an old wreck in the adjacent River Plym estuary ('The Laira') I notice that shags and cormorants are nesting. The AWS bell rings clear and we head off for Hemerdon. I make a quick check in the engine room to see if there are any faults, but everything seems fine. Back in the cab speed is down to 32 mph on the steepest part of the bank, but the amps are rather high at 2,200. However, despite the wet rails and blowing leaves there is no slipping. On the night of its fateful run in 1983 50041 nearly stalled here on icy rails; it if had, might it have avoided the spectacular derailment at Paddington? As built, the Class 50s had tractive effort control so that drivers could regulate power more precisely to prevent slipping and thus drive with more confidence. The AWS again rings clear, this time signifying that we are approaching the summit loops.

50002 is running well, and we canter down Rattery bank and take the through road at Totnes, where we pass 50009 'Conqueror' on the 0635 Bristol to Plymouth. Coseting through the station power is applied for the assault on Dainton, but the AWS goes for a 20 mph track slow. I take another good look around the engine room and find a small coolant leak, but it is not severe enough to warrant the loco being taken off its duty. As we slog up the incline 31264 rolls downhill with a special freight for the Royal Naval Dockyard: later in the day the interloper ventured even further west, being put on a Railfreight turn to St. Blazey. Back at Dainton we enter the tunnel at 42 mph and on 2,000 amps.

Down the other side we go, dropping past Stoneycombe Quarry (which is quiet today) and on towards Aller Junction. This is well and truly lower quadrant country, but not for much longer: the year is 1985, and this is the start of the last remaining pocket of semaphore signals on the Great Way West to Plymouth. At Newton Abbot West Box we draw to a stand before the signal clanks off to allow us onto the down relief road. 'Superb' runs round, couples up, and we receive the right away for the Paignton branch. Snaking over the 10 mph crossovers I tell the driver that I will ring Laira on arrival to inform control that the loco is able to continue its diagram on the 'Torbay Express' to London. The driver and guard are booked through to Taunton.

The train ambles along the branch in the heavy drizzle towards the seaside – not that the beaches will be crowded today. I am dropped off at Paignton platform, while '02 continues to Goodrington Sidings in order to run round. 50020 'Revenge' is waiting in the up platform with the 1010 to Plymouth. I make my tea and report to Laira, also telling them that '20 is on my return train, 'Revenge' being restricted to local working for observation at this time.

Once again I join the driver in the cab of a Fifty.At 1005 the engine is started, disturbing the seagulls. The crossing gates go down, the horn is sounded, and we make a spirited start out of the resort. Climbing the bank out of Paignton the amber wheelslip light comes on, and with speed at 45 mph power is eased. Stone bridges pass by as the curving tracks wind their way towards Torquay. Although colour light signals are in evidence the semaphores remain in use, in the final few months of their lives.

Few passengers await our train at Torquay, where on the other line 31417 runs in on an Exeter to Paignton local. '20 gets on the move again, but the AWS alarm sounds for a stretch of new track: the driver is not quick enough cancelling it and so the brakes go on, speed dropping to 20 mph. Passing Aller Junction we run side by side with 50036 'Victorious' on the 0730 Penzance to Aberdeen. '36 will take No. 4 road under the wall, as it is non-stop (this area has now been terraced over to make a car park). We are cautioned under amber signals into Platform 3.

Before 50020 runs round I notice the lampman refilling the oil supply for the signal lamp wicks. We wait for a while to connect with the 0845 Paddington to Penzance HST. Today the service is headed by power car 43002 'Top of the Pops', and the set includes executive saloon 40513 used for transporting VIPs. We follow the HST out to Aller Junction, and, when the signal clears, 'Revenge' is opened up to tackle the climb to Dainton Tunnel.

Autumn leaves blow around to show that the weather is drying up. With the summit in sight, the track ahead from the driver's window looks like a great hump through the tunnel bore. We can see that the signal on the far side is on, and the repeater on the tunnel mouth sounds as we plunge into the gloom. With the brake on the train slows to a crawl, which continues all the way into Totnes. The HST does not stop there but we do, and so afterwards the route is clear. Rattery is the last main climb of my journey, and I talk to the driver about the old days and trackmen. At one time trackmen on the up line at Marley Tunnel (twin bore and of cosmetic use only, located near the summit at Wrangaton) would drive a wooden stick into the ground near the tunnel mouth and attach an old rag to it, which would flap as a train approached and thus warn them to stand clear.

Inside the tunnel the pinpoint of light grows steadily larger, and the driver tells me to watch the trackside as we leave the tunnel. With the train pushing the air out of the single bore at a great rate the trees and shrubs are blown violently as we emerge.

Another twenty minutes and we pull in to Plymouth, on time. '20 now has to remove the first three coaches and attach them to rear of the 0932 Penzance to Paddington 'jumbo' as it arrives. In readiness we run out to Plymouth west end and wait; it is not long before the jumbo hoves into view in the care of 50033 'Glorious'. The job completed we return to Laira shed: the South Devon banks have been tamed for another day.

Day Return to Penzance

It was a warm summer's afternoon, the date sometime in 1975 or 1976. After booking on at Laira at 1430 I was told I was to take the stopper to Penzance, in order to monitor 50002, which was suffering from engine stopping faults. The loco had just been transferred from Old Oak Common, and typically for the machines not long off the LMR, it was in a rather gruby condition. Of course, at the time '02 was unnamed and unrefurbished. After obtaining tools and tea can I made my way to No. 6 road where the loco stood outside the shed, ready for its booked turn, 2C74, the 1645 off Plymouth.

The cab interiors were in a poor state, dirty and showing some corrosion to the desk fittings, possibly indicating that the loco had lain out of use for a long time. The reason became obvious when I entered the engine room, as a new main generator had recently been fitted at Crewe Works. Before setting off I checked the levels of coolant, engine sump oil and engine governor oil. The four character headcode was still operational, and when I confirmed the train reporting number with the crew this was rolled up to order. The engine was started and final checks made. There was time in hand, and so the driver suggested we move off shed early and make a cup of tea at North Road station.

The 1645 was usually made up of five coaches, and was primarily used by schoolchildren and shoppers from East Cornwall. It called at all stations, including the Halts at Dockyard, Devonport, Keyham and St. Budeaux, and then all points west. The guard's whistle blows and we pull out on time. 50002 ambles along past the Naval dockyard, where I notice a large collection of surface ships and submarines, all with names but as yet no association with the Fifties. On towards the Royal Albert Bridge spanning the River Tamar; a brake application is made to bring our speed down to the required 5 mph. Half way across and we are in Cornwall.

There is no sign of any faults yet, but I don my earmuffs and disappear into the engine room to observe as power is applied after the Saltash stop. Oil pressure remains steady at 60 psi. The heat thrown out from the engine is breathtaking, with the exhaust pipes glowing cherry red: one set of pipes is white hot, indicating the engine timing is out, a point to be booked. All the turbocharges are working together at 9 psi. As yet there is nothing to indicate the cause of the shutdown problem, and so I go out past the dirty inertia air filters and take in the fresh, cool air.

We continue our journey westwards, running into the setting sun, which suggests it will be a fine day tomorrow. Arrival at the Penzance terminus is scheduled for about 7 pm, and we approach the station a few minutes down. I resolve to inform Laira of the position on arrival, as the next leg of '02's diagram is 1A01, the 2135 up sleeper throughout to Paddington. We are greeted by the station supervisor who says we are to take 50035 back with us in multiple as far as Plymouth, as it is suffering a low power fault which will need to be rectified at Laira. It is agreed that we will run round to the flower bay under the sea wall and collect '35 and then couple on to 1A01 before having our tea break. The Penzance Class 08 pilot shunts the train, and then the pair of Fifties (connected in multiple) back on and their engines are shut down. Now it's time for tea.

I decide to go around both locos and check all oil and coolant levels prior to departure. By now the sun has sunk into the Atlantic, and the passengers are on board for their nocturnal journey to the Metropolis. We ease out of the station gently with theoretically 5,400 bhp and a trailing load of twelve for 470 tons. 50002's engine shuts down; we restart and I go into the engine room. The engine stops again. A second restart is made and we struggle into St. Erth. I inform the driver that it appears to be an electrical fault now that we are working in multiple. We therefore decide to uncouple the multiple jumper cables, using '35 to provide the ETH only and '02 for traction. '02 picks up its train with a struggle, now pulling an extra 117 tons as well as the heavy train. Fortunately there is no more trouble from 50002, and so there must be a jumper fault on one of the locos.

The problem now is that we are losing time. As our secondman is a passed Class 50 driver the decision is taken to use '35 for tractive power but driven from its own cab; in other words working the Fifties in tandem, not in multiple. Now it is right away to Plymouth with no further mishaps, '02 working well and '35 limping on its low power. At last Devon is reached, and as we pass Saltash we have a clear view of the Royal Albert Bridge all lit up. The night is clear and starlit, and this gives reflections in the water at the dockyard. On the final approach to Plymouth the signal is against us and we stop, before the yellow aspect shines and the route indicator displays Platform 7. We are fifteen minutes down. Our duo are detached whilst 50004 waits patiently in Platform 8 to take 1A01 forward. We slip out of the lights of North Road station and I get ready to see our duty foreman and then sign off.

Mike with the nameplate from 50014 ''Warspite', the loco having been cut up over a year previously.

Mishaps with the Milk

Trains of milk from the West Country to London ceased in 1980: the sight and sound of the distinctive six-wheels tankers squealing round the sharp curves in Cornwall is very much a thing of the past. Now the traffic goes by road. Some would call it progress.

Three incidents with milk trains come to mind, separated by over fifteen years. Firstly we go back to 1963 and the severe winter of that year. It was sometime in March and I was nearing the end of my turn on the early shift at Old Oak Common when a call for help came in from the Unigate Dairy at Wood Lane in White City. The trouble turned out to be a pair of Class 43 'Warships'. D818 'Glory' and D862 'Viking', which were booked on the 1440 empty tanks to the St. Erth creamery but were unable to reverse into the sidings. In fact both were assigned for repair and were travelling home to Laira for attention.

My route home out of London passed close by, and so I was asked to fix the recalcitrant hydraulics and then travel forward on them to Greenford. It did not take long to diagnose the fault, and the milk train was able to set off only thirty minutes late.

Many years later, after the hydraulic 'Warships' had all been scrapped and I had been reallocated to Laira, two breakdowns on the milk took place.

On this particular Sunday afternoon a cool wind was blowing. Our depot was very quiet: not a hammer or spanner could be heard. I was one of only two fitters assigned to this shift. Examples of Classes 46, 47 and 50 were stabled, dormant, all around. At about 6.30 pm the phone rang with the news that 50036 on the Kensington milk had become derailed at Totnes while backing into the siding to collect further full tankers. That was the end of the peace and tranquillity, and the depot was transformed into a hive of activity. The 'on-call' breakdown foreman arrived, as did the night rerailing gang. It was the early hours of the following morning before they all returned, bringing 50036 in for repair (the breakdown train loco having been used to take the milk forward).

When the Fifties arrived from the LMR the St. Erth to Kensington milk service became the preserve of the Class 52 'Westerns', since no heating was required. After their demise the ETH-fitted 50s were frequently used, along with the more appropriate 47/0s. On this particular day 50017 was allocated to the up service, whilst I had the job of accompanying unnamed 50013 plus 50042 on the 1023 stopper from Plymouth to Penzance, both locos being on the test. During the Truro stop the station supervisor came up to us and said that '17 had refused to start and needed rescuing. Arrangements were made for '42 to be detached at St. Erth to take charge of the 1610 service to Kensington, with '13 continuing alone for the last few miles to Penzance.

The milk train crew were waiting for us as we run up to the signal box at St. Erth; 50042 is quickly unhitched and makes its way to the milk siding and the stricken 50017. I decide to travel back on the milk, and when the train is ready I stop for a tea break. Sitting on a bench on the station platform in the sunshine I watch as 50013 rumbles in with an up passenger. Our driver informs me that we will follow '13 up the line, stopping off at Lostwithiel to pick up more tankers. This we duly do, and while the dead Fifty is transferred to Laira and I sign off, the milk rumbles on in to the night in order that Londoners can have something to put on their cornflakes.

Today we have been booked on a planned recovery operation, following the derailment the previous day of part of a Meldon Quarry stone train at Bow, on what was left of the 'Withered Arm' network of LSWR lines. The wind was blowing hard, it was decidedly cold, and there was sleet and rain to contend with too. Snow and freezing temperatures had been forecast for later on. We were all kitted up with hats, overalls, boots and thick winter coats – it felt like we were off for a day in a labour camp. There was no sign of the train, and so a suggestion was made the one of us ring Laira to find out if it had set off yet. On doing so the reply was that it was just about to leave, as they were awaiting the arrival of one member of the gang who lived in Cornwall. It be another twenty or so minutes before it reached Ivybridge.

A busman's day out

It may seem rather odd that a railwayman should choose to spend his day off travelling the metals, but this particular journey was a rather special one. The famous Settle and Carlisle line was under threat of closure, and a special being run from Plymouth seemed an ideal opportunity to ride this magnificent route before it was lost for ever.

So it was that a group of friends and I boarded the F&W 'Scenic Settler' shortly before the 4 am departure one cold and frosty morning in April 1984. The open-plan Mark 1 coaches had windows running with condensation, but this at least promised that we would be warm for the day ahead. Just before the head count we nipped to the front of our train to see what motive power had been provided by Laira. Why, it was my favourite, 50008 'Thunderer'; how thoughtful!

Under frosted sleepers our 1Z49 special slips out of Plymouth. The journey north and east is uneventful, and mostly a chance to catch up on the lost sleep. Beyond Bristol, though, the talk was of the Lickey Incline, which today had a speed restriction at the start of the climb: perhaps the assistance of the bankers – usually a pair of Class 37s – would be called for. It seemed so, for the train slowed on the approach to Bromsgrove, at the foot of the bank; but then the train crew realised that no bankers were on duty this Saturday, and so the Fifty would have to haul the heavy load on its own.

'Thunderer' lived up to its name as it took full power for the ascent, and made a spirited attack on the stiff gradient. Even so, speed gradually fell to walking pace, and we all began to wonder if '08 would stall. At last the special clawed its way over the summit at Blackwell, the loco having given its all. We gave a cheer: the Laira Fifty was in good fettle – as, of course, is only to be expected!

'08 was now in its native region, the LMR, and soon we arrived under the wires at Birmingham New Street. From there 1Z49 made its way to Bescot Yard, and as we gently ran through we catch sight of the virtually brand-new 56113 and 58010. We then rejoin the WCML and '08 treated us to a fast sprint to Crewe, from where it is to be relieved by a Class 47. Crewe had been D408's base from new, and this was the second time it had been back since its transfer to Laira a decade previously. The other occasion had also been on a railtour from Plymouth, when in November 1979 the unrefurbished and freshly repainted 'Hoover' took a trainload of railfans to the Works Open Day.

As '08 retired to the depot to join the other varied products of English Electric's Vulcan Foundry (not far up the line, at Newton-le-Willows), 47537 'County of Gwynedd' backed onto our train.Appropriately enough the Brush was allocated to Crewe Diesel depot. As it got stuck in to the journey north, we are told that we are to travel the S & C from north to south, since two other specials were to use the route in the opposite direction.

Carlisle is reached some twenty minutes late, but there was still time for a lunch stop. Then we were away again, and quickly onto the S & C metals at Petteril Bridge Junction. The weather was most uninviting: bitterly cold with frequent sleet showers, yet still with the odd snatch of sunshine. As we approach Lazonby the first of the northbound specials is passed, hauled by EE stalwarts 40009 and 40033. Despite the weather the scenery is breathtaking, with Cross Fell, Ingleborough and Penyghent capped in snow. As we breast the summit of the long climb at Ais Gill the talk is of the other excursion, which is reported to be steam-hauled, by either LNER A4 'Sir Nigel Gresley' or SR West Country 'City of Wells'. We catch a glimpse of the old turntable at Garsdale, complete with fencing to stop locos being spun around in the gales. In the event it was the latter that filled our open coach windows with steam as we slowed for a photographic stop at Dent. The signal box there now looked decidedly derelict, but there is no time to investigate as the stewards soon shepherd us back on board. At Blea Moor two Class 31s, 31152/209, are stabled but with engines running. Then we cross the majestic Ribblehead viaduct: would this be for the last time? Heading down into the foothills we take the freight-only branch from Hellifield to Blackburn, and pass by the Clitheroe cement terminal, where the last surviving Clayton Type 1 is still employed as a shunter; but it was not on view today.

By now 50008 must be getting ready to leave light engine for Stockport, where it will take charge of 1Z49 once more. We thread our way through Blackburn and Manchester Victoria, and catch sight of more Class 40s at Miles Platting before taking another freight branch, the Ashton Moss North Junction spur into Stockport. 'Thunderer' was there waiting, and after the usual photographing the Laira loco heads for home.

For me this 18-hour railtour to the S & C was a most enjoybale 'busman's day out'. Since then, Class 50's have themselves traversed the line on excursions; and happy to relate, the route has now been reprieved and can enjoy a bright and secure future. Maybe one day our preserved 50 will delight the railfans as it pounds up the 'Long Drag' and through the desolate moors, just as 'City of Wells' did on our day out.

Freshly painted 50017 'Royal Oak'

The road to the Scilly Isles

Even though there are no railways on the Scilly Isles, perhaps 50014 'Warspite' was attempting to get there one hot day in July 1984 when it derailed itself in the Scilly Isles flower bay at Penzance. Even being named after a nuclear submarine did not seem to have helped. Instead, a call was made to Laira for the breakdown unit to attend.

As part of the team I was detailed to help with the rerailing of the stricken 'Warspite'. 47334 was provided for the breakdown train, and we made steady progress westwards, arriving at the Cornish terminus at 10 am. The temperature was already in the 80s. Firstly we walked over to the loco to estimate the damage and how long it would take to put the 117-ton beast back on the rails. No. 1 bogie, at the London end, had dropped fully off the road: it would have to be raised up to above rail height and then moved across so that the flanged wheels could be lowered on to the rails.

The sweat was already on our brows as we unloaded the equipment – jacks, rams, packing etc. An appreciative crowd of holidaymakers on the sea wall and platforms watched our efforts as we worked solidly without a tea break in order to beat the heat of the day. The first lift failed to get the wheelset clear of the rail, and so we had to have a second attempt, by repacking under the wheels before lowering and removing the jacks to have another go. This being completed successfully, the next move was to use the rams to align the wheelset over the 4'8 1/2" gauge, and then gently lower the loco back on to the road.

During this operation the 'Scillonian', the steamship that plied the route from the Scillies to Penzance, berthed at the nearby jetty and began to unload its cargo of flowers, potatoes and tomatoes. These would be sent forward to the Midlands and London in the first place via 3S15, the 1225 perishables and parcels service to Glasgow (just as soon as '14 had cleared access to the rail loading bay).

Once our work was complete and we had cleared up, the foreman told us that we had a couple of hours spare before a suitable path back to Plymouth became available. The sea looked very inviting, and so some of the lads took a swim, while the rest sat on the sea wall eating hot Cornish pasties fresh from the bakers. We all had a good laugh, the local womenfolk wolf-whistling at the sight of railway workers stripped to their underpants. At 4 pm the 'Scillonian' set sail for the Scillies, and a little later the breakdown train trundled slowly back towards Laira, with 50014 at its head.

My verdict: a good breakdown although rather sunburnt.

Old rivals meet again

Let's go now to events surrounding the Laira Open Day on Saturday September 7th 1985. This story begins two days earlier, when I am sent to the Dart Valley Railway at Buckfastleigh to prepare D1023 'Western Fusilier', GWR tank 4555 and a Victorian coach for transit to Laira, where they will be put on display.

The preheating on D1023 is started up, and a light fire raised on the 45xx; the train is marshalled with the 'Wezzie' at the front, as this will haul the others down to Totnes. When everything is ready a well-earned tea break is taken on board my old hydraulic friend.

Meanwhile at Laira 50025 is also prepared for duty, plus a train of Mark 1 coaches to help with braking. The 50 will pull us on the BR lines from Totnes since preserved diesels are not permitted to work under their own power on the main BR network. We set off down the remains of the GWR Ashburton branch and wait in the refuge siding for the Fifty.

At about 1.30 pm 50025 greets its old rival D1023 on the Western Region mainline. The 'Western' is shunted behind the 'Hoover' , and soon the signalman gives us the road for the journey to Laira. Camera-laden enthusiasts are everywhere, photographing the first 50/52 combination to storm Rattery Bank in many a long year. Both diesels have their engines running; this is indeed a sight and sound to savour.

The trip passes without any hitches, as does the highly successful Open Day. On the Monday after the operation has to be reversed, with the honour of train loco this time failing to 50013, which required a trial run due to low power problems.The hydraulic and the steamer were made ready, and mineral wagons added to the formation for braking. D1023 renewed its association with Hemerdon Bank, but soon it was a case of saying farewell to the DVR locos at Totnes as they returned to the more sedate lifestyle of preserved locos.

Today both 50013 and 50025 have been scrapped, while D1023 lives on in preservation. We must all work together to ensure that at least one Fifty can say hello to D1023 in retirement.

Withdrawn 50041 and further down 50021 are dumped by the side of the mainline.

Testing by night

Once again it is my turn on the night shift, this time working on the collision damage to 08645. After finishing off the job of replacing the buffers it is 0230 and time for a tea break. The foreman approaches me and says my next job is to take a pair of Fifties on a trial run. I had earlier noticed 50029 and 50041 coupled together outside on No. 6 road, engines running.

Laira is busy getting the trains ready for the morning as I walk out to examine the locos. 'Renown' had just undergone an 'E' exam plus repaint, whilst 'Bulwark' had been receiving attention for overloads; both now needed to cleared for an unrestricted return to traffic. The driver arrives, and soon we make our way to the dummy signal at the shunt neck. It is a clear night, but the moon and stars do little to illuminate '29's cab, which is lit only by the instrument lights. At least the cab heating works well. We get the signal and set off light engine, '41 leading, the 5,400 bhp on tap quickly accelerating us to 60 mph before Tavistock Junction Yard, where the brakes go on to bring us to a stand.

With ear protectors on I go into the engine room, and observe as the power is applied for the charge at Hemerdon Bank. I take a good look around, checking the fault boards and making notes. At the summit my mate signals from '41's back cab that all is OK, and so I shutdown '29's engine in order that 'Bulwark' can be assessed alone. Once more we roar off into the night. Approaching South Brent and also Marley Tunnel I notice the headlights of road traffic on the A38 dual carriageway. Before descending Rattery 'Renown' is restarted, and with the locos again paired in multiple we drop down towards Totnes. The AWS sounds for a yellow signal and is cancelled, the brakes going on hard. I look out of the cab window and can see sparks flying from the brake blocks on both 50s, this only adding to the spookiness of the night. There is a 20 mph speed restriction in force due to new track, but we are brought to a stand anyway at the next signal.

After a few minutes the signal clears and we gently ease into Totnes. The station is in darkness but the adjacent milk depot is all lit up and bustling with activity; the clock shows the time as being 0430. With the locos idling, the crew change ends. I chat to my mate, who pronounces 50041 as fine for re-entering traffic. From the signal box comes the sound of Dainton calling to Totnes to accept a train, and it is not long before an unidentified Fifty thunders past on the down through road with a heavily laden sleeper train. Once it is away we cross over from the up to the down through line and move forward to colour-light signal T100, which fills the cab with its baleful red glare. We have to wait for the sleeper to clear the section to Rattery, which seems to take an inordinately long time.

This time '29 will do all the work, and so '41 is shut down.I resume my position in the engine room when we get the road at last, and conclude that although the amps and field diversions are spot on there is some more work to be done on 50029 before it can have the all clear. We glide down Hemerdon at 60 mph, speed still rising until the brakes are applied at Tavistock Junction. I note that the Class 08 shunter has already arrived at the yard there for its day's work in the sidings. We are then quickly on to Laira Ocean Siding signal, which is quite a tall one, and showing a single yellow aspect with seven white feathers to the left, indicating we are to leave the mainline. A Fifty is crossing out of Laira Carriage Sidings with Waterloo line stock: it is the green machine, 50007, and so the Southern Region will be pleased today.

By now dawn has broken, and waterfowl are feeding on the mudflats of the Plym estuary. We crawl into the depot yard and come to a stand. 'Renown' is shut down, and I sign off and go home to bed.

White gold of Dartmoor

It seems like only yesterday that the little old 13-ton clay hoods were an everyday part of the West Country railway landscape. These wagons were used to transport kaolin (china clay) from pit to port in Cornwall, and also to the Staffordshire potteries. As we shall see, they helped to transport some of the clay extracted from Dartmoor too. It was the tent-shaped blue tarpaulin covering that gave them their distinctive appearance, though it could not have been especially efficient at keeping the clay dry.

Living in Ivybridge, on the edge of the Dartmoor National Park, I would often take a walk out to the railway line armed with a camera. One of my favourite trains was 6V70, the 0424 Stoke-on-Trent to St. Blazey 'Clayliner' which returned empty wagons from the potteries. For a while it regularly turned up in the West Country with a Class 50 in charge. On two days a week, at about 4.30 pm, the train would stop to drop off some empty hoods at the siding at Ivybridge, where a local company was responsible for filling a handful of wagons with clay from a pit on the Moor. The clay was brought in by lorry and the wagons loaded one at a time by conveyor in a special shed, ready for next day's 'Clayliner'.

On this particular day it was damp and misty, far from ideal for photography. The light level inexorably dropped as I waited in the cold. At last the unmistakeable sound of a Fifty booming around the Dartmoor foothills filtered through the mist. The siding was empty so I guessed that it would call, and sure enough the train was clearly slowing as it swung round Ivybridge viaduct, spanning the River Erme, and past the remains of the station platforms. Slowly it crept up to where I was waiting, 50014 providing the power. The shunter alighted and waved the train on past the points; a manoeuvre which was awkward in both up and down directions since the line curved sharply, cutting off the line of sight.

The shunter phoned Plymouth Panel Box to release the token for access to the siding, and then '14 slowly propelled its long train back off the mainline. Another Fifty could be heard approaching on the up line; the gloom was pierced by the loco's high-intensity headlight, and with an exchange of blares on their horn 50035 surged by with 3S15, the 1210 Penzance to Glasgow parcels. As 'Ark Royal' hurried eastwards towards South Brent, five wagons were uncoupled from 6V70, and then the shunter climbed back into '14's cab. The Clayliner resumed its journey as 'Warspite' powered away into the Devonshire dusk.

Ivybridge was now quiet; not a sound could be heard.I strolled home, ready by now for a hot cup of tea. Alas, this trip could not be repeated now: Ivybridge siding closed in 1986; 50014 hauled its last train 1987; and the last of the clay hoods was scrapped in 1988.

Saturday night, Sunday morning

It is a cold winter's night at Laira, a Saturday, and my seventh consecutive night on duty. Thankfully there will be no more night shifts for me for a fortnight after this. Nothing untoward happens until during our midnight tea break the call comes through that a Fifty and its civil engineers train are off the road in Exmouth Junction Yard.

Our duty chargeman takes a head count of breakdown crew on duty: fortunately there are six of us, and so no off-duty staff need to be roused from their beds. Also, a quick getaway is to our advantage since the sooner we go, the sooner we can get back – it could well be a very long shift indeed. This time it is a road journey, as Laira has now been allocated a Bedford/Bruff road/rail vehicle. Within minutes we are away, zipping up the A38 to Exeter in the pitch darkness. I look at my watch: 0045 on Sunday morning. It is a time for reflection as to what the rest of the night is going to bring. Although the Bruff is very cosy, it is bitterly cold outside: this is not likely to be the most pleasant of jobs.

Leaving the dual carriageway we make our way through the streets of Exeter, observing the drunks and the taxis, the drivers of which no doubt wondering what on earth we are doing here. Away from the city centre the street lights are switched off, and we have to navigate by shining the Bruff's headlights off the street nameboards. Finally we come to the old wagon shops of the LSWR at Exmouth Junction. It is years since I have last been here; no doubt if it had been daylight I could have observed how derelict this once vital loco shed and works had become.

Carrying handlamps and wearing our luminous jackets we alight and in a ghostly procession try to locate the derailed train. The buildings and yard appear to have been abandoned for a long time, and we cannot see or hear anything. It is suggested that we make for the signal box, a beacon of light some distance away. Hacking through nettles and brambles we chance upon a Permanent Way ganger, and question him as to the whereabouts of the derailment. "Over in the siding by the mainline", he replied, then added in a puzzled voice, "where's your train?" Our foreman pointed across the yard and told him it was the road vehicle with its headlights on. We now had to ascertain how best to get the Bruff over to the vehicle and the driver cautiously made for the right spot, bumping along at walking pace. The ground is very soft, due to coal dust, but we manage to park fairly close by. The gangers also arrive en masse in their transit van.

While the others start unloading, three of us plus the foreman walk over to the train to estimate the job in hand. The loco on this occasion is 50037, resplendent in Network South East colours but at this time allocated to the DCWA (Departmental) sector. At least it is being employed on the correct type of duty, the train having been starting out for Topsham on the Exmouth branch to assist with reballasting work. The damage is not too severe; 'Illustrious' remains on the rails, but the first loaded stone hopper has left the road and in so doing locked its buffers with the wagon behind. The remaining ten hoppers are alright, but of course are trapped in the siding until the cripple can be rerailed.

Our gang get to work, speeded on by the chilling cold.We cut away the drag links on the wagon, allowing '37 to be started up and moved clear. An hour's hard graft and the miscreant wagon is back on the rails. After the breakdown gear is clear of the lines '37 again splutters into life and couples up to the wagon before removing it to another siding. The gangers make a start on repairing the damaged sleepers so that the rest of the train can then be released. Tired and weary we clear up the site and then are free to make the homeward journey.

It is 0530: not many folks are about this time on a Sunday morning. Our Bruff requires fuel and so we pull into a 24-hour service station. I think the owner was quite amused at the sight of six grubby rail staff buying the Sunday papers; but that's life!

'Indomitable' off the rails

It was a dull, overcast Monday morning and I was working on 50001, berthed in Laira's No. 4 road. My name came over the tannoy to report to the foreman's office: a Fifty was off the rails at Penzance again, trapping in other locos, and I was needed to help with the rerailing. The culprit this time was 50026, allocated to Old Oak Common.

The breakdown gang assembles, and 47217 (based at Immingham) backs onto the special rerailing stock. It is 0745 when we get underway, our train being given the reporting number 1Z99. The morning rush hour is building up in Plymouth, and even the rail traffic in North Road station is at a standstill as we pass. We brew up and have breakfast as we roll over the Royal Albert Bridge; a tug towing barges passes by underneath. The Cornish countryside is frosty, and the chimneys of cottages emit smoke from freshly lit fires. Many pheasants patrol the hedges and fields.

At Burngullow 37247, complete with 'Cornish Railways' logo, waits in the sidings on a rake of clay hoods; it will shortly take them up to Drinnick Mill for loading. Truro finds 37230 in the yard on cement tanks, presumably en route to the little depot at Chacewater. As we travel westwards the sun tries to break through. Once we reach Long Rock everyone is on their feet, looking out of the windows. 50026 is spotted off the road beside the sea wall, in virtually the same spot as 50014 back in the summer. Somehow I don't think we will be taking a dip today, though.

47217 parks us in No. 4 road, alongside '26, which has No. 2 bogie completely off. Behind the Fifty are 45124 and 50048, unable to leave the flower bay until '26 is righted. It is 1020 when we start work, fitting the special Class 50 bodyside lifting jacks and then placing traversing beams across the damaged tracks. Inch by inch 'Indy' is manoeuvred back on to the rails; but just as we are nearly there the bogie tilts back-wards. The rear wheels will not lift any higher because the bodyside jack is at full height. It is decided to jack under the bodyframe near the rear wheels to tilt the rear bogie forwards again, and thus allow the wheel flange to rerail itself. From then on it does not take long to finish off, spurred on by the smell of cooking wafting from the mess van and carried on the salty sea breeze.

Penzance station has carried on its normal business as we worked. 47121 was given the job of hauling 3S15, the 1225 Glasgow parcels service standing at Platform 3, while 50029 pulled into Platform 2 with the 0701 stopper from Exeter. Overhead helicopters take off from the nearby heliport on the Scilly Isles run.

Once 50026 has been checked for damage and the track gauge measured for any irregularities we can then tuck into our hot dinner. Suitably nourished, the gang clears up the equipment while I start '26's engine and perform a power check with the driver. 'Indy' will take us home as train 9Z99 – the code for a breakdown – and 47217 will stay at Penzance as a spare loco.

St. Michael's Mount is shrouded in sea mist as we pull out a suitable length of time behind the 1355 Bristol stopper. Our homeward journey is a slow one, giving me plenty of time to notice the old Cornish tin mines around Redruth and the primroses and gorse that are just bursting into flower on the embankments. '26 behaved itself, and the Plymouth outskirts are reached just as the evening commuter rush begins. The Monday blues have now gone; the Tuesday blues will not be long in coming.

Back at Laira '26 is stabled on No. 1 road in order to be lifted on the big jacks for an inspection of its underside. It shouldn't be out of traffic for long.

Dogfish adrift

Rerailing jobs are interesting, but on some occasions the predictability of shed work seems far preferable. It certainly did at 0530 one winter's morning as I stood beside the line at Ivybridge with a couple of colleagues, waiting to be picked up by the breakdown train.

Today we have been booked on a planned recovery operation, following the derailment yesterday of part of a Meldon Quarry stone train at Bow, on what was left of the 'Withered Arm' network of LSWR lines. The wind was blowing hard, it was decidedly cold, and there was sleet and rain to contend with too. Snow and freezing temperatures had been forecast for later on. We were all kitted up with hats, overalls, boots and thick winter coats – it felt like we were off for a day in a labour camp. There was no sign of the train, and so a suggestion was made the one of us ring Laira to find out if it had set off yet. On doing so the reply was that it was just about to leave, as they were awaiting the arrival of one member of the gang who lived in Cornwall. It be another twenty or so minutes before it reached Ivybridge.

We hung around restlessly, the wind rattling the corrugate sheets of the clay loading shed roof. Finally in the distance the piercing headlamp of a Fifty could be seen. 50037 passes us and draws to a halt. Very cold and already weary we climbed aboard to join the rest of the conscripts, perking up when we found that hot tea and buttered toast was on the menu. '37 sets off towards Exeter, but has to stop at Newton Abbot so that the boiler on 'Puffing Billy', the steam-operated breakdown crane, can be checked. The crane-man stokes the fire so that there will be plenty of steam when we reach the site.

At Exeter St. Davids we are informed that '37 will have to be taken off for a mainline duty. The train is shunted into Riverside Yard, just as dawn begins to break. It is now starting to snow. The talk is mainly about the weather, and also our Cornish workmate who did not show up. Puffing Billy is keen to start work as it starts to blow off at the safety valves. Half an hour passes and then we are on the move again, curving left at Cowley Bridge Junction and onto the Barnstaple branch – Southern metals, as was. 'Illustrious' is still hauling us after all. A rather abrupt halt is made at Crediton station, and we are greeted by our missing colleague, who had driven over the Moor from Cornwall.He said that the road conditions were treacherous up on the edge of Dartmoor, where it was snowing hard.

Somewhat to our surprise '37 is detached and runs back past us light engine, disappearing back towards Exeter. We consume coffee and biscuits in the silence, before investigating what is happening. It seems that the Fifty is indeed required elsewhere, and a replacement loco was being found. Another half an hour ticks by before help arrives in the shape of 31259. It is decided to reassemble our train with the crane at the front and loco at the back, which will then have to push us up the single line to the breakdown site.

Finally this is made ready, and we are at last heading for Bow. The Class 31 is working hard on the curves and stiff gradients. Most of us look out of the windows at the snow-covered scenery. A very low and narrow stone overbridge is sighted up ahead, with railway road vehicles parked around it in the lane. We slow to a stop, us workers getting out with the foreman to survey the damage. Five laden 'Dogfish' stone wagons lie drunkenly snaked across the rails. These need to be sorted into ones that can be removed today, and ones for scrapping or heavy repair and unable to travel, which will need to be recovered on another day with the aid of a long-wheelbase flat wagon.

Down comes the driving snow and sleet as we manoeuvre the steam crane into position for the nearest wagon. The first list is to move the 'Stokes bogie', one of which needs to be attached to each end of the crane for stability. Luckily at Bow there is plenty of room for the operation as in steam days the route had been double track. The lifting chains are attached and the bogie swung to one side, the wagon being just within the radius of our crane jib.

The next few hours are taken up with rerailing one dogfish at a time, and in between having to reposition the crane. Each wagon is lifted to one side and swung around to be put on the rails at the rear. Four dogfish are rescued in this way, ready to be towed back to Exmouth Junction shops for repair. Only one remains, but this is beyond repair and will be left on site for now. We are all feeling hungry, and the smell of cooking from our van announces that it is time for a meal break. Bangers, mash and beans for starters, followed by fruit cocktail and custard, all washed down with lots of hot tea. As we tuck in, the PW gang set to with repairing the track.

Not surprisingly, we are loath to move after this feast; the weather is not exactly welcoming, but the winter daylight is short and we cannot afford to delay. It is virtually dark by the time we finish, and when the Stokes bogie has been rerailed and the site cleared up there was no trace of daylight left. As the wintery moorland night closed in we left the Withered Arm and headed back for Laira, dropping off our mate at Crediton en route, and then the three of us at Ivybridge. Home was reached, more than a little exhausted, fourteen hours after setting out.

50003 'Temeraire' 50004 'St.Vincent', the latter had been withdrawn a fortnight previously.

Class 50 Society

The Class 50 Society is the oldest and largest interest group for followers of the class. Through its bi-monthly magazine **"CLASS 50 FORUM"** it keeps members fully informed of developments concerning the class and also carries feature articles and photographs.

The society has a preservation fund for donations and also manages its own share appeal which will enable shareholders to participate in the purchase of a Class 50.

For full details of society membership, the share scheme and a free magazine send two first class stamps to :-

CLASS 50 SOCIETY,
PO Box 31,
WESTON SUPER MARE;
Avon.